D0190492

Great Food Made Simple

John Topham

The Perfect Combination

John Topham

Great food made simple...

All of these recipes are firm favourites of mine, and I love to cook them at home.

At The General Tarleton, in my home county of Yorkshire, we believe in creating fantastic flavours from the best local ingredients. And that's the simple philosophy behind these dishes. They're easy to prepare, and I've made them all using Lamona appliances – so I know you'll get great results.

Although my work is all about food, I also do plenty of home cooking, and I can heartily recommend the Lamona range. It offers lots of choice for cooks of all kinds – whether you're an experienced chef or a novice in the kitchen.

When you've got your new Howdens kitchen installed – complete with Lamona appliances – try cooking these recipes and they may become family favourites for you too!

⚡ Lamona & John Topham
The Perfect Combination

Simple Starters

Family Favourites

Mains to Impress

Desserts and Cakes

Essentials

Simple Starters

Whether you're entertaining guests or feeding the family, you want to create a good first impression – which is easy with these tried and tested recipes.

Little Money Bags with a Shellfish Sauce

Little Money Bags with a Shellfish Sauce

Fresh seafood, herbs and vegetables, all wrapped in a pastry parcel with a creamy lobster sauce. This is my signature dish at The General Tarleton, and I hope you'll see why.

Serves 4 30 mins preparation, 15 mins cooking

Ingredients

4 sheets of Fleur de Bric pastry or filo pastry

1 tablespoon olive oil

50g leeks, courgettes, and yellow and red peppers – cut into thin strips

50g salmon fillet, skinned

50g cod fillet, skinned

50g halibut fillet, skinned

8 Queenie scallops

50g fresh prawns

12 tarragon leaves

4 long chives

Salt and pepper

Shellfish Sauce

150ml white wine

2 shallots, very finely diced

Juice of ½ lemon

415g tin lobster bisque

150ml double cream

200g unsalted butter, diced

To make the Shellfish Sauce

1. In a heavy bottomed pan, add the white wine, shallots and lemon juice. Heat gently to reduce by half.

2. Add the lobster bisque and reduce by half. Add the double cream, and again reduce by half.

3. Turn down the heat and gently whisk in the diced butter. Keep the sauce in a warm place until you need it.

To make the Money Bags

1. Preheat the oven to 180°C/gas mark 4.

2. Heat the olive oil in a pan or wok, and stir fry the vegetables until they just start to soften. Remove them from the pan and allow to cool completely.

3. Blanch the chives in boiling water for 10 seconds. Refresh in chilled water.

4. Cut the fish into ¼ inch cubes. Take one sheet of pastry, and put a few pieces of each fish in the centre. Then put two scallops, some prawns and a mound of vegetables on top of the fish. Season with salt and pepper, and add some tarragon leaves. Carefully lift up the outside edges of the pastry, crimp them together above the fish mixture and secure with a chive strip.

5. Bake in the oven for 12-15 minutes, until the pastry is golden brown and the seafood is cooked.

6. Put the Money Bags on warm plates, and pour the Shellfish Sauce around each one.

Queenie Scallops

Queenie Scallops

Fresh scallops are always a treat. This dish makes a lovely starter with warm, crusty bread.

Serves 2   15 mins preparation, 8-10 mins cooking

Ingredients
24 Queenie scallops
200g butter
3 cloves garlic, finely chopped
Lemon juice
200g medium Cheddar, grated
100g Gruyere, grated
2 tablespoons breadcrumbs
Salt and pepper

4 x King scallop shells for serving, or 4 shallow dishes

1. Preheat the oven to 180°C/gas mark 4.

2. Start by clarifying the butter. To do this, melt it gently in a pan and scoop off any solids that form on the surface. Carefully ladle the clear melted butter from the milky liquid, and keep it to one side until you need it.

3. Divide the scallops between the four shells or dishes. Add the chopped garlic to the clarified butter, and pour a tablespoon of this garlic butter over each portion of scallops, followed by a squeeze of lemon. Lightly season with salt and pepper.

4. Sprinkle the Cheddar over the scallops, followed by the Gruyere, then the breadcrumbs.

5. Keep them in the fridge until you need them. Cook for 8 minutes on the top shelf of the oven, or until golden.

Spiced Hearty Vegetable Soup

Satisfying and nutritious, this substantial soup makes a tasty starter. The spices add a rich depth of flavour without overpowering the vegetables.

Serves 4   15 mins preparation, 30 mins cooking

Ingredients

1 onion

1 leek

3 carrots

2 sticks celery

1 sweet potato

1 clove garlic, crushed or finely chopped

100g dried red lentils

1 litre chicken or vegetable stock

1 tablespoon coriander seeds

1 tablespoon cumin seeds

½ teaspoon dried chilli flakes

2 tablespoons olive oil

1. Peel and chop all the vegetables into evenly sized, small pieces.

2. In a small frying pan, dry fry the coriander and cumin seeds for a couple of minutes until you can smell their aroma. Put the seeds into a pestle and mortar, and grind into a rough powder.

3. Put the olive oil into a large pan (with a lid), then add the onion and cook gently until soft, but not brown.

4. Add the remaining vegetables. Put the lid on the pan and cook gently for 10 minutes, stirring occasionally.

5. Add the lentils, garlic, crushed coriander and cumin seeds, then the chilli flakes, followed by the stock. Simmer gently for 20 minutes, or until the vegetables are soft. This soup should be quite thick, but as the lentils swell and soak up the liquid with cooking, it may start to become too thick. If so, just add a little water while it's still simmering.

Spiced Hearty Vegetable Soup

Steamed Mussels with Ginger, Lemongrass and Coconut Milk

Steamed Mussels with Ginger, Lemongrass and Coconut Milk

The freshness of the lemongrass, ginger and coriander, combined with the slight heat of the chillies, gives an interesting Asian twist to mussels. This is an impressive starter if you're entertaining.

Serves 4 15 mins preparation, 5 mins cooking

Ingredients

2kg fresh, cleaned mussels
1 small onion, finely chopped
2 cloves garlic, crushed
1 stick lemongrass, very finely chopped
1 tablespoon fresh ginger, chopped
2 mild red or green chillies, seeded and chopped
150g coconut milk (without sugar)
200ml white wine
1 bunch coriander, coarsely chopped
Splash of oil for cooking

1. Heat the oil in a very large pan with a fitted lid (mussels shouldn't be more than four deep so use two pans if necessary). Fry the onion until it starts to soften and go slightly transparent. Add the garlic, lemongrass, chillies and ginger, and cook for two minutes.

2. Add the mussels, white wine and coconut milk. Put the lid on, turn up the heat and boil for 4-5 minutes.

3. Remove from the heat and discard any mussels that haven't opened. Serve the mussels in large bowls with a generous helping of the sauce. Sprinkle with chopped coriander.

Family Favourites

If you like to keep your food informal and don't want to use every pan in the kitchen, these recipes will inspire you to produce appetising main courses with very little effort.

Beefburgers

Homemade beefburgers are always a huge hit. I enjoy adding a dollop of spicy relish to mine – or bacon, or cheese... the opportunities are endless.

Serves 4 15 mins preparation, 15 mins cooking

Ingredients

1 small onion, peeled and finely chopped

400g minced beef

2 cloves garlic, crushed or finely chopped

1 egg yolk

25g fresh breadcrumbs

2 tablespoons mixed fresh herbs, chopped (parsley, chives and tarragon are ideal)

Ground black pepper

1 tablespoon soy sauce

Olive oil

To serve

Crunchy lettuce, finely shredded

1 beef tomato, thinly sliced

1 red onion, thinly sliced

Mayonnaise (optional)

4 burger buns

Salt and pepper

Chips

1. Fry the onion in a little olive oil until it's soft but not browned. Leave to cool.

2. Mix all the other ingredients in a bowl. Add the cooled onions and shape into four evenly sized burgers. Leave in the fridge for at least an hour (although they will keep for longer).

3. Preheat the oven to 200°C/gas mark 6.

4. To cook, fry the burgers in a shallow pan with a little olive oil, for a few minutes on each side. Once they've browned, place in the oven for 10 minutes, or until they've cooked through.

5. To serve, slice the burger buns in half. Mix the shredded lettuce with a little mayonnaise, season with salt and pepper, and divide between the four buns. Add a slice or two of tomato to each, place the cooked burgers in the buns, and top with a slice or two of red onion.

Beefburgers

Chilli Con Carne

Chilli often tastes better the day after you've made it. So if you're pushed for time, this is a great dish to prepare in advance. To create a real Mexican feast, you can serve it with homemade guacamole and salsa.

Serves 4 15 mins preparation, 45 mins cooking

Ingredients

500g minced beef
1 large onion
1 large carrot
1 red pepper
1 stick celery
2 large cloves garlic, crushed
150g mushrooms
2 x 400g tins tomatoes
410g tin kidney beans
198g tin sweetcorn
1 red chilli, very finely chopped
1 teaspoon chilli powder (to taste)
1 dessert spoon cumin seeds, ground to a powder
Salt and pepper
A dash of olive oil

To serve

Coriander
Soured cream
Fresh guacamole and salsa (see page 74)
Rice or tortilla wraps

1. Start by chopping all the vegetables, apart from the mushrooms, into small cubes. In a large casserole dish, fry the onion in olive oil for a few minutes, or until soft.

2. Add the minced beef, and fry until browned.

3. Add the carrot, pepper, celery, red chilli and garlic. Stir, then add the chilli powder, ground cumin, salt and pepper. Add the tinned tomatoes and bring to a simmer.

4. Rinse the tinned kidney beans, add and simmer for 30 minutes. Check the seasoning and adjust if you need to, as the strength of fresh chillies can vary.

5. Slice the mushrooms and add to the casserole dish with the sweetcorn. Simmer for a further 20 minutes.

6. Garnish with coriander and soured cream. Serve with fresh guacamole and salsa, and rice or tortilla wraps.

Chilli Con Carne

Meatballs in Tomato Sauce

Meatballs in Tomato Sauce

Homemade meatballs in a homemade sauce – this is comfort food at its very best. I like to dish it up on a chilly day, with plenty of steaming pasta.

Serves 6 20 mins preparation, 1 hr cooking

Ingredients
500g minced beef
500g minced pork
75g breadcrumbs
1 heaped tablespoon oregano
1 egg yolk
1 sprig rosemary, finely chopped
1 tablespoon dried chilli, finely chopped
1 teaspoon cumin powder
2 tablespoons olive oil
100g fresh mozzarella
Salt and pepper

For the Tomato Sauce
4 x 400g tins chopped tomatoes
A generous splash of olive oil
2 fat cloves garlic, finely chopped
2 teaspoons oregano
1 tablespoon red wine vinegar

To serve
Pasta
Fresh Parmesan cheese, grated

1. In a large bowl, mix all the meatball ingredients together (apart from the mozzarella and olive oil). Once they're well mixed, roll into balls – about the size of a golf ball.

2. In a large frying pan, heat the olive oil and brown the meatballs all over until they're nicely coloured.

3. To make the tomato sauce, warm the olive oil in a large casserole dish. Add the tinned tomatoes, garlic and oregano, and simmer very gently for about an hour. Add the red wine vinegar to the tomato sauce and stir.

4. Preheat the oven to 200°C/gas mark 6.

5. Place the meatballs in the tomato sauce and cook in the oven for about 45 minutes.

6. About 10 minutes before the meatballs are ready, thickly slice the mozzarella and place it on top of the meatballs, letting it melt in the remaining cooking time. Serve on top of pasta with grated fresh Parmesan.

Shepherd's Pie

Everyone loves shepherd's pie. You can make this recipe as an everyday stand-by for the family, or serve it as an easy supper for guests.

Serves 4 15 mins preparation, 1 hr cooking

Ingredients

1 tablespoon olive oil
450g lean minced lamb
3 large carrots, finely chopped
1 large onion, finely chopped
1 teaspoon tomato purée

1 tablespoon fresh thyme, chopped
300ml lamb stock (hot)
900g potatoes
50g butter

1. Heat the olive oil in a large pan. Add the onion, cook gently for a few minutes, then add the carrots. Cook on a low heat for five minutes.

2. Add the mince and cook until coloured, using a spoon to break up any lumps.

3. Add the hot lamb stock, thyme and tomato purée, and simmer without a lid for approximately 35 minutes. You want to reduce the liquid, but make sure it doesn't become too dry.

4. Preheat the oven to 180°C/gas mark 4.

5. Peel, cut and boil the potatoes until soft, then mash them with the butter.

6. Spread the mince into a gratin dish and cover with the mashed potato. Cook in the oven for approximately 20 minutes, until golden on the top and piping hot in the centre.

Shepherd's Pie

Italian Sausages with Puy Lentils

This is a good alternative to traditional bangers and mash. If you can, invest in quality sausages from your local butcher, and serve with a glass of Italian red wine.

Serves 4 15 minutes preparation, 45 mins cooking

Ingredients

200g pancetta

300g puy lentils

1 large onion, peeled and finely chopped

3 sprigs thyme

1 bay leaf

2 cloves garlic, crushed

1 tablespoon tomato purée

1½ litres chicken stock

8 good quality Italian sausages

1. Preheat the oven to 180°C/gas mark 4.

2. In a large casserole dish, gently fry the pancetta until it's brown and turning crispy. Add the onion and cook for about 5 minutes, until soft but not brown.

3. Add the garlic, bay leaf, thyme and tomato purée, and give everything a good stir before you add the lentils. Finally, add the stock and simmer for 20 minutes.

4. Place the sausages in a roasting dish in the oven, and cook for 20 minutes. Turn them occasionally to ensure they brown evenly.

5. Check the consistency of the lentils and reduce further, or add more liquid if you need to. Once the sausages are cooked, add them to the lentils and simmer for 5 minutes before serving.

Italian Sausages with Puy Lentils

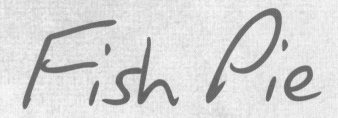

Fish Pie

A fish pie makes an ideal family dinner. With this recipe, you can prepare the pie in advance, and put it in the oven at the last minute. It's good to serve with plenty of fresh, green vegetables.

Serves 6 10 mins preparation, 1 hr cooking

Ingredients
400g salmon fillet, skinned
400g white fish (such as cod, haddock or halibut), skinned
250g prawns, peeled
1 onion, peeled and sliced
1 bay leaf
75g plain flour
75g butter
850ml milk
1 handful of parsley, chopped (keep the stalks separate)
Salt and pepper

For the mash
750g potatoes, peeled and cut into small pieces
50g butter
100ml double cream

3-litre gratin dish

1. Preheat the oven to 180°C/gas mark 4.

2. Boil the potatoes in lightly salted water until soft. Drain and mash.

3. In a small pan, gently heat the cream and butter. Once melted, beat them into the mashed potatoes, season and keep to one side.

4. Put the onion, bay leaf and parsley stalks into a large shallow pan. Add the milk, then bring to the boil and simmer. Add the salmon and white fish, and poach for 8 minutes.

5. With a slotted spoon, remove the fish and flake into a gratin dish, checking for bones. Strain and keep the cooking liquid.

6. Melt the butter in a medium-sized pan, then stir in the flour to make a smooth paste. Keep stirring for four minutes, gradually adding the cooking liquid a little at a time, and stirring well after each addition. Once you've added all the liquid, cook the sauce on the lowest heat for 10 minutes. Add the chopped parsley and prawns to the sauce, then pour it over the cooked fish.

7. Spread the mashed potato evenly over the top. Cook for 35 - 40 minutes, until bubbling and golden.

Fish Pie

Chicken Masala

Chicken Masala

When you make a curry from scratch you really get to enjoy all the Indian spices, flavours and aromas. It's well worth the effort.

Serves 8 20 mins preparartion, 1 hr 15 mins cooking

Ingredients

12 chicken thighs, boned, skinned and cut in half
25g unsalted butter
400g tin chopped tomatoes
500g chicken stock
2 tablespoons tomato purée
2 small onions, finely chopped
4 cloves garlic, crushed
1 aubergine, peeled and diced
40g root ginger, peeled and finely chopped
200ml coconut milk
2 small red chillies, finely chopped
Juice of ½ lemon
30g toasted flaked almonds
1 large bunch coriander, chopped
Salt and pepper

Spices

1 tablespoon cumin seeds
1 teaspoon fenugreek seeds
1 dessert spoon paprika
2 teaspoons curry powder
1 pinch saffron
1 dessert spoon turmeric
¼ cinnamon stick
1 pinch curry leaves
1 teaspoon cardamom seeds
1 teaspoon mustard seeds
1 teaspoon garam masala

To serve

Basmati rice

1. For two minutes, heat all the spices in a large pan, moving them around so they don't burn. Remove and grind them in a pestle and mortar.

2. Season the chicken. Add the butter to the pan you used for the spices, then add the chicken and brown it all over. Remove from the pan.

3. Put the onions, garlic, ginger and chillies in the pan and cook for 2-3 minutes. Add the aubergine, tinned tomatoes, tomato purée, chicken stock, chicken and spices, and simmer gently for 45 minutes.

4. Check the seasoning and the consistency of the sauce. It should be reasonably thick. If it's not, reduce further (by simmering or boiling the liquid so the water evaporates). If it's too thick, add more stock or water.

5. Add the coconut milk and lemon juice. Simmer for a further five minutes, then sprinkle with chopped coriander and flaked almonds.

6. Serve with basmati rice.

Roast Chicken Salad with Avocado, Watercress and Lemon Mustard Dressing

Roast Chicken Salad with Avocado, Watercress and Lemon Mustard Dressing

This combination of slow-roasted chicken, fresh crisp salad and creamy dressing works really well – and although it takes a little time, it's quite straightforward to make.

Serves 6 15 mins preparation, 1 hr 30 mins cooking (excludes resting time)

Ingredients

A 2kg free range chicken
2 lemons, sliced
2 dessert spoons clear honey
150ml white wine
1 dessert spoon Dijon mustard

4-5 tablespoons thick mayonnaise
2 small shallots, finely chopped
2 bunches watercress
1 crisp lettuce, chopped
2 ripe avocados, sliced

1. Preheat the oven to 200°C/gas mark 6.

2. Place the chicken on its side in a greased roasting tin. Roast for 15 minutes. Turn the chicken onto its other side and roast for another 15 minutes.

3. Put the chicken on its back and pour the honey over it. Add the white wine and lemon slices to the tin. Reduce the heat to 180°C/gas mark 4, and cook for a further 30 minutes. Baste the chicken with the juices. Reduce the heat to 140°C/gas mark 1, and cook for 30 minutes more.

4. Lift the chicken into a dish and leave to cool. When it's cooled, carve into slices.

5. Strain the roasting juices into a pan, skim off any fat and simmer to reduce by half. Whisk in the mustard and mayonnaise to make a thin, creamy dressing.

6. In a large dish, mix the crisp lettuce, watercress and shallots. Add the avocado and sliced chicken. Pour over the dressing to serve.

Mains To Impress

Creating that 'wow' factor is all about interesting combinations of flavours. You'll find plenty of them here, in recipes that guide you through the preparation in simple steps.

Seared Fillet of Seabass with Tomato Tart, Rocket and Pesto

Seared Fillet of Seabass with Tomato Tart, Rocket and Pesto

Seabass is often the highlight of a restaurant menu, but it's easy to cook at home too. Its sweet, white flesh goes perfectly with the tomatoes in this recipe.

Serves 2 20 mins preparation, 25 mins cooking

Ingredients

2 x 200g seabass fillets
1 roll puff pastry
2 dessert spoons tomato purée
4 plum tomatoes
Olive oil
Ground black pepper
25g butter
Salt and pepper

To serve

Rock salt
Fresh lemon juice
Small packet of rocket, washed
100g good quality pesto – or use my homemade recipe (see page 76)

1. Preheat the oven to 180°C/gas mark 4.

2. Take the roll of puff pastry and use a saucer to cut out two large discs. Place the discs on a piece of greaseproof paper, then place another layer of greaseproof paper on top and sandwich between two baking trays to stop the pastry from rising. Bake in the oven for 15 minutes, or until golden. Once cooled, you can keep the pastry in an airtight container for up to a week.

3. Skin the tomatoes by crossing the bottom of each one lightly with a small knife, then placing them in a large bowl and covering with boiling water. Leave for 12 seconds. Then, using a spoon, take the tomatoes out of the hot water and plunge them into cold water. Carefully peel off the skin, then slice.

4. Take each pastry disc and spread 1 dessert spoon of tomato purée over each. Arrange the sliced tomatoes on top. Season with salt and pepper, and add a light drizzle of olive oil. Bake in the top of the oven for 8-10 minutes. (Note: you can time the cooking of the tarts to go with the fish.)

5. Heat a frying pan, then add a tablespoon of olive oil followed by the seabass, skin side down. Cook for 5-6 minutes, add a knob of butter and cook for a further minute. Turn the fish over and cook for 3 more minutes. Remove from the heat and leave to rest in a warm place.

6. To serve, place each pastry tart in the centre of a plate. Put the rocket on top, followed by the seabass. Drizzle the pesto around the rim of the plate. Finish the fish with a squeeze of lemon juice, a little olive oil and a pinch of rock salt.

Fragrant Moroccan Spiced Lamb and Couscous Salad

Fragrant Moroccan Spiced Lamb and Couscous Salad

Serves 4 20 mins preparation, 40 mins cooking

Ingredients

2 racks of lamb (ask your butcher for it French trimmed and with most of the fat removed)

Moroccan rub

1 teaspoon black peppercorns

1 dessert spoon cardamom seeds, husked

1 dessert spoon cumin seeds

1 dessert spoon coriander seeds

¼ stick cinnamon

1 star anise

½ teaspoon dried chilli flakes

Zest of 1 lemon

2 cloves garlic, crushed

1 teaspoon fresh coriander, chopped

1 dessert spoon fresh ginger, chopped

4 tablespoons natural yogurt

1 pinch rock salt

For the Couscous Salad

250g couscous

400ml boiling water

Olive oil

50g sunblushed tomatoes

50g toasted pinenuts

8 sprigs mint, chopped

12 sprigs coriander, chopped

Juice of 1 lemon

1 Granny Smith apple, cored and diced

¼ cucumber, diced

4 spring onions, thinly sliced

1. Dry-fry the cardamom, cumin, coriander, cinnamon, star anise and black peppercorns for one minute, then grind in a pestle and mortar. Mix the spices with the remaining ingredients and smear over the lamb. Marinate for 2 to 12 hours.

2. Preheat oven to 180°C/gas mark 4.

3. Roast in the oven for 35 minutes for pink lamb, or longer if required. Rest for five minutes in a warm place before carving.

4. In a large bowl, pour the boiling water over the couscous, add one tablespoon of olive oil, cover with cling film and leave for five minutes. Add all the remaining ingredients to the couscous. It should now look fluffy, having absorbed all the water.

5. Serve the couscous salad on a plate, add the carved lamb and drizzle with olive oil.

Pork Savoyard

This dish looks very impressive when you serve it – and with the Gruyere, ham and potatoes, it makes a really satisfying meal.

Serves 4 15 mins preparation, 30 mins cooking

Ingredients
400g pork fillet escalopes
4 slices ham
150g Gruyere, grated
200g spinach
4 medium potatoes
200g butter
1 tablespoon olive oil
Salt and pepper

To serve
Tomato Sauce for Pasta (see page 80)

1. Start by clarifying the butter. To do this, melt it gently in a pan, and scoop off any solids that form on the surface. Carefully ladle the clear melted butter from the milky liquid, and keep it to one side until you need it.

2. Peel the potatoes and grate them onto a clean tea towel. Wrap the towel around the grated potato and squeeze it over the sink to remove as much starch as possible.

3. In a medium frying pan, add half the clarified butter, then the potatoes. Using a spoon, press the potato into a smooth, round, flat shape and cook gently for 10-12 minutes.

4. Carefully turn the potato out onto a plate and add the remaining clarified butter to the pan. Cook the other side of the potato for the same amount of time. Once cooked and golden on both sides, remove the potato from the pan. Put it in a heat-proof dish and keep it in the oven on a low heat.

5. Put the olive oil in a hot frying pan, and sear the pork escalopes for two minutes on each side. Remove them from the pan and place on top of the potato.

6. Now turn your grill to high, as you'll need it shortly. While the grill is warming up, use the same pan you cooked the pork in to cook the spinach for a couple of minutes, until it's wilted. Season with salt and pepper and squeeze any excess liquid from it.

7. Place the spinach on top of the pork, followed by a layer of sliced ham and the grated Gruyere over the top. Place under the grill until the cheese has melted. Serve with some of my Tomato Sauce for Pasta (see page 80).

Pork Savoyard

Pot Roast Belly Pork braised in Cider

Pot Roast Belly Pork braised in Cider

Belly pork is becoming more and more popular in restaurants, and it's a great cut of meat to cook at home. It's excellent value for money – and when you cook it slowly in cider, it's extremely tender. Roast roots go with it perfectly.

Serves 5 15 mins preparation, 2 hr 45 mins cooking

Ingredients
1.2kg belly pork, stripped of skin and bones
1 heaped tablespoon fennel seeds, toasted
Zest of 1 lemon, grated
1 bunch sage, to taste
1 bunch thyme, to taste
1 pint good quality cider

For the roast roots
2 red onions
2 white onions
1 bulb garlic
4 large carrots
1 butternut squash
Half a celeriac
Thyme, to taste
Sage, to taste
3 tablespoons rapeseed oil
Salt and pepper
1 pinch sugar

1. Preheat the oven to 190°C/gas mark 5.

2. Lay the belly pork (meat side up) on a chopping board, spread the fennel seeds, lemon zest, thyme and sage evenly over the meat. Season with salt and pepper, then roll up tightly and tie with string.

3. Place in a roasting pan and cook in the oven for 30 minutes.

4. Turn the oven down to 160°C/gas mark 3 and pour the cider into the roasting pan. Cook for a further 2 hours. Remove from the oven and keep in a warm place to rest for 10 minutes before you start to carve.

5. While the pork is cooking, prepare the roast roots. Peel and chop the vegetables into similar sized chunks. Place in a roasting tin, and toss with the rapeseed oil. Season with salt, pepper and sugar, and cook in the oven at 160°C/gas mark 3 for 45 minutes, until everything is tender and lightly caramelised.

6. Serve the vegetables, and place the carved pork on top, drizzling with the braising juices.

Breast of Chicken rolled in Parma Ham with Melting Brie

This is a great dish for entertaining. It looks good, never fails to impress, and yet is surprisingly easy to cook. It's a handy recipe to have for special occasions.

Serves 4 15 mins preparation, 35 mins cooking

Ingredients

4 skinless chicken breasts
4 large slices Parma ham
100g brie
25g butter
Juice of 1 lemon
1 dessert spoon fresh thyme, chopped
100ml cream
400g penne pasta
A dash of olive oil

1. Place one chicken breast on a board. Gently lift the fillet away from the breast without removing it.

2. Using a sharp knife, make an incision under the fillet to form a pocket. Fill it with a quarter (25g) of the brie, then press the fillet back down on top.

3. Cut a large sheet of cling film and place a piece of Parma ham on top. Put the filled chicken breast onto the Parma ham, roll it firmly around the chicken and wrap it tightly with the cling film. Store in the fridge and repeat this process with the other three chicken breasts. Leave to set in the fridge for two hours before cooking.

4. Preheat the oven to 180°C/gas mark 4.

5. In a frying pan, heat the butter. When it's bubbling, add the chicken breasts (having removed the cling film). Brown each side, then place on a baking tray and cook in the oven for 25 minutes.

6. Bring a large pan of water to the boil, add salt and a dash of olive oil. Add the pasta and cook until 'al dente' (still slightly firm).

7. Strain the cooked pasta, and return to the pan. Add the lemon juice, thyme, cream and any roasting juices from the chicken. Gently stir in the sauce, divide between four plates and put the chicken on top.

Breast of Chicken rolled in Parma Ham with Melting Brie

Breast of Chicken with a Spicy Chorizo Risotto

You can't rush a risotto – it needs a bit of time and patience to cook. So preparing this dish is a good way to unwind, while you enjoy all the delicious aromas it produces.

Serves 4 20 mins preparation, 40 mins cooking

Ingredients

4 small chicken breasts
200g chorizo, skinned and sliced
1 bunch coriander, chopped
3 cloves garlic
1 small onion, finely diced
150ml white wine
800ml chicken stock
30g butter
2 tablespoons olive oil
1 pinch saffron
1 red chilli, finely chopped
250g risotto rice
Lemon juice

1. Preheat the oven to 180ºC/gas mark 4.

2. Warm a large frying pan, then add the butter. Once it's bubbling, add the chicken breasts and brown each side for 2-3 minutes.

3. Place the chicken on an oven tray and bake for 25 minutes, until firm and golden.

4. While the chicken is cooking, you can make the risotto. Heat the chicken stock in a pan. Once it's boiling, reduce the heat, and leave it to simmer gently.

5. Take a large sauté pan and cook the sliced chorizo for two minutes, until it's slightly coloured and the oil melts away from it. Remove the chorizo from the pan and keep warm, leaving the oil. Add the onion to the chorizo oil, and cook for one minute, stirring continuously. Add the garlic and rice.

6. Once the rice is coated with the oil, add the white wine and increase the heat, stirring occasionally until the wine has absorbed into the rice. Now add the saffron and the hot chicken stock, a ladle at a time, stirring after each addition. Wait until each ladle of stock is absorbed before you add the next. This process takes about 20 minutes.

7. Once you've added all the stock and the rice is cooked, add the chorizo, chilli, lemon juice and coriander, along with any juices from the chicken roasting pan.

8. Divide the risotto between four plates and place the chicken breasts on top.

Breast of Chicken with a Spicy Chorizo Risotto

Desserts and Cakes

You may like your puddings wholesome and
fruity, or perhaps you simply want to satisfy a
sweet tooth. Either way, there are recipes here
to keep everyone happy.

Apple Coble Cake

Apple Coble Cake

This really tasty, wholesome cake is best eaten as a pudding, warm with a generous helping of double cream and a dusting of cinnamon. The name comes from a type of boat, found in Scotland and the North East of England. It's flat-bottomed – just like the cake!

Serves 8 15 mins preparation, 40 mins cooking (excludes cooling time)

Ingredients

4 eggs

130ml vegetable oil

500g caster sugar

1 pinch salt

250g plain flour

10g ground cinnamon

1 teaspoon bicarbonate of soda

1 teaspoon baking powder

450g carrots, finely grated

70g walnuts, chopped (optional)

3 Bramley cooking apples, peeled and chopped

To serve

Double cream

A dusting of cinnamon

2 x 25cm diameter cake tins, greased and floured

1. Preheat the oven to 180°C/gas mark 4.

2. Beat the eggs at high speed in a food mixer until they're light and frothy. Reduce the speed and gradually add the vegetable oil. Turn the mixer to low and add 400g of the caster sugar and salt.

3. Sift the flour, cinnamon, baking powder and bicarbonate of soda, and slowly fold into the mixture, followed by the carrots and walnuts.

4. Divide the cake mixture between the two cake tins and bake for around 40 minutes, until the cake springs back when you press it lightly in the centre. Leave to cool on a wire rack.

5. In a heavy bottom pan, cook the apples with the remaining 100g of sugar and a little water, until soft. Leave them to cool. Spread the cooked apple on one of the cakes, then put the other cake on top to make a sandwich.

6. To warm up a slice of the cake, put it on a plate and microwave it for 1 minute. Serve it with the cream and a dusting of cinnamon.

Auntie Bertha's Biscuits

Auntie Bertha's Biscuits

These crunchy, satisfying biscuits are a family recipe. They are quick and easy to make – and great as a mid-morning or afternoon snack. Perfect with a cuppa.

Makes 30 Biscuits 20 mins preparation, 10 mins cooking

Ingredients

150g self-raising flour
150g porridge oats
175g caster sugar
7g bicarbonate of soda
150g butter
58g golden syrup

1. Preheat the oven to 160°C/gas mark 3.

2. Line a flat baking tray with greaseproof paper.

3. Measure the flour, oats and sugar into a bowl. Melt the butter, golden syrup and bicarbonate of soda gently in a pan, then pour them over the flour, oats and sugar and mix together.

4. Roll small amounts of the mixture between the palms of your hands to make small balls, and place them on the baking tray. Press each one lightly with a fork to flatten slightly before baking in the oven for 10 minutes, until golden in colour.

5. Carefully transfer the biscuits from the baking tray to a wire rack. Let them cool before storing in an airtight container.

Eton Mess

Eton Mess

This simple, light dessert is perfect for a warm summer's evening. It was traditionally served at Eton College's annual cricket game against the students of Winchester College.

Serves 4 20 mins preparation

Ingredients
4 large meringues (shop-bought ones are fine)
250g raspberries
250g strawberries
135ml double cream, softly whipped
275ml natural yogurt
2 tablespoons caster sugar
Juice of 2 limes

1. Place half the raspberries in a food processor with the sugar and lime juice. Pulse to a purée, then pass through a fine sieve to make a coulis.

2. Remove the hulls and halve the strawberries, and place in a large bowl. Add the remaining raspberries, large chunks of the meringue, whipped cream and yogurt. Mix gently.

3. Pour the raspberry coulis over the top. Fold once or twice with a spoon so you can still see the coulis in a ripple effect in the meringue mixture.

4. Serve in four large glasses.

Lemon Surprise Pudding

The 'surprise' of this pudding is the way it stays soft underneath the set surface. It's a lovely, indulgent consistency – you only have to slide your spoon in to find out...

Serves 4 - 6 20 mins preparation, 40 mins cooking

Ingredients
100g butter
250g sugar
4 lemons, juice and grated zest
4 eggs, separated
100g self-raising flour
300ml milk

2½ pint (1½ litre) oval pie dish

To serve
Fresh pouring cream

1. Preheat the oven to 180°C/gas mark 4.

2. Beat the butter in an electric food mixer. When it's softened, add the lemon zest and sugar, and beat well. Add the egg yolks one at a time, and beat well. Sift the flour and fold into the mixture with the milk and lemon juice.

3. In a separate bowl, whisk the egg whites to form stiff peaks. Then fold them into the lemon mixture. The mixture will look a bit lumpy at this stage – but don't worry, it doesn't need to be perfectly mixed.

4. Pour into the pie dish and bake for 40 minutes.

5. Remove from the oven and cool for a few minutes. The pudding should be well risen and set on top, but still wobbly underneath. Serve with fresh pouring cream.

Lemon Surprise Pudding

Mia's Chocolate Cake

Mia is my wife's grandmother, and this recipe has been handed down from her. For celebrations of any kind, it's always a winner. Once you've put the icing on top, you can either serve it as it is, or be as creative with the cake decorations as you like.

Serves 10 15 mins preparation, 45 mins cooking

Ingredients
150g self-raising flour
175g caster sugar
175g soft margarine
75g drinking chocolate powder
3 large eggs
3 tablespoons boiling water

1 x 18-20cm round tin, greased and lined

For the milk chocolate icing
60g butter
250g icing sugar
1 tablespoon cocoa powder
3 tablespoons hot milk
2 drops of good quality vanilla essence

1. Preheat the oven to 160°C/gas mark 3.

2. Put all the cake ingredients into a large bowl and beat (slowly at first) for 2 minutes. An electric mixer is ideal.

3. Pour the mixture into the tin and bake in the centre of the oven for 45-60 minutes (depending on your oven). The cake should be well risen and firm. Once cooked, leave the cake in the tin for a few minutes, then turn it out onto a wire rack to cool.

4. To make the icing, melt the butter in a pan, and blend in the cocoa powder. Then stir in the icing sugar, milk and vanilla essence, and beat until smooth and thick. Slice the cake horizontally in two. Spread half the icing between the two halves as a filling, and the other half on top of the cake

5. Decorate the surface of the cake as desired (shown with chocolate shavings).

Mia's Chocolate Cake

Prune and Armagnac Soufflé

Prune and Armagnac Soufflé

You make the dish in three stages: the Armagnac-soaked prunes (these are a dish in their own right), the prune purée, and finally the soufflé. You can make the soaked prunes and purée well in advance.

Serves 4 30 mins preparation, 10 mins cooking

For the Armagnac-soaked Prunes
1kg de-stoned prunes
400ml Armagnac
120ml water
120g caster sugar

4 ramekin dishes

For the Prune Purée
500g Armagnac-soaked prunes
35g cornflour
100ml Armagnac
100g caster sugar
50ml water

For the Soufflé
25g unsalted butter
150g caster sugar (plus extra for ramekin dishes)
6 egg whites
8 Armagnac soaked prunes
4 tablespoons prune purée
Icing sugar for serving

Armagnac-soaked Prunes

1. Heat the sugar and water in a pan until boiling. Simmer for two minutes to make a syrup.

2. Place the prunes in a storage jar, pour the Armagnac and syrup over them, and store for at least a week (they will keep for up to a year in a sealed jar).

Prune Purée

1. Blend the prunes in a food processor.

2. Heat the sugar and water in a pan until boiling. Simmer for two minutes to make a syrup.

3. Dissolve the cornflour in the Armagnac. Add this and the syrup to the prunes and blend again. Store in a sealed jar until you need it (it will keep in the fridge for up to a week).

Soufflé

1. Preheat the oven to 180°C/gas mark 4.

2. Grease the ramekins with butter. Sprinkle the extra sugar around the dish so it sticks evenly to the butter.

3. Whisk the egg whites using an electric whisk or mixer. Once they're forming soft peaks, add the caster sugar a little at a time, whisking after each addition.

4. In a separate bowl, mix the prune purée with a third of the meringue mixture. Then, carefully fold in the remaining mixture.

5. Half fill each ramekin, place a prune on top of the mixture then fill with the remaining soufflé mix. Using a palette knife, press the soufflé mixture into each ramekin and scrape off any excess to leave a smooth, flat surface. This is important to ensure the soufflés rise evenly. Use a piece of kitchen paper to wipe around the rim of each ramekin.

6. Bake for 8-10 minutes, until well risen and golden. Serve with a prune on top of each soufflé, dusted with sieved icing sugar.

Rhubarb Crumble

Rhubarb Crumble

You can serve this classic British pudding warm or cold. I like it the traditional way, with custard, but it's also good with double cream or ice cream.

Serves 4 15 mins preparation, 35 mins cooking

Ingredients
600g rhubarb
Juice of 1 orange
100g sugar
¾ stick cinnamon

For the crumble
¼ stick cinnamon
50g butter
80g plain flour
60g caster sugar
30g blanched almonds, toasted
Zest of 1 orange, grated

1. Preheat the oven to 180°C/gas mark 4.

2. Wash and chop the rhubarb into 2cm slices. Place in a pan with the sugar, orange juice and ¾ of the cinnamon stick. Gently bring to the boil and add more sugar if necessary (although remember you are adding a sweet crumble).

3. Once the sugar is melted, remove from the heat. Take out the cinnamon stick, and transfer the rest to a gratin dish.

4. For the crumble, grind the remaining ¼ of the cinnamon stick to a powder, using a pestle and mortar.

5. Place the butter, flour and sugar in a food processor and blend to breadcrumb consistency. Crush the toasted almonds by hand and add to the crumble with the powdered cinnamon and orange zest.

6. Spread lightly and evenly over the rhubarb, without pressing. Bake for 30-35 minutes.

Sticky Toffee Pudding

Sticky Toffee Pudding

If you've never tried to make this at home before, now's your chance to see how easy it is. As with all baking, the quantities of each ingredient are crucial – but if you get those right, you'll have a new favourite in your repertoire of dishes.

Serves 6 20 mins preparation, 25 mins cooking

Ingredients
57g butter
175g caster sugar
1 egg
300ml boiling water
1 teaspoon bicarbonate of soda
227g self-raising flour
170g dates, chopped
1 teaspoon baking powder

For the caramel sauce
150g brown sugar
150g double cream
150g unsalted butter

6 x 150ml metal pudding pots, greased and coated on the inside with caster sugar

1. Preheat the oven to 180°C/gas mark 4.

2. For all the mixing and beating in this recipe, use an electric mixer. Mix the butter and sugar until pale and creamy. Add the egg and beat well.

3. Combine the baking powder and flour, sieve and fold into the batter mixture. Mix the dates with the bicarbonate of soda, pour the boiling water over and blend well. Add this to the batter and mix in thoroughly.

4. Divide the mixture between the six pots, and cook for 20-25 minutes until risen, golden and firm to touch.

5. In a heavy bottomed pan, heat all the sauce ingredients and stir until the sugar has dissolved.

6. Turn out the puddings onto plates or bowls and pour the caramel sauce over.

Will's Steamed Treacle Sponge Pudding

This is my son Will's all-time favourite pudding. He makes it himself, and has created this recipe – it's the best version of a classic favourite.

Serves 4 20 mins preparation, 1 hr 30 mins cooking

Ingredients

2 tablespoons golden syrup

110g soft brown sugar

110g butter (or margarine)

55g self-raising flour

55g wholemeal flour

1½ teaspoons baking powder

1 dessert spoon black treacle

2 large eggs

1½ pint (850ml) pudding basin, well buttered

1. Spoon the golden syrup into the buttered pudding basin.

2. Sieve the flour into a large mixing bowl, then add the remaining ingredients and beat well for two minutes.

3. Spoon this mixture onto the syrup in the pudding basin, and smooth the surface so it's even.

4. Cover the basin with a double layer of kitchen foil, with a pleat in the middle to allow for the pudding to rise. Tie the foil firmly in place with string. Put the basin into a steamer over boiling water and steam for 1½ hours.

5. To serve, turn the pudding out onto a plate. If you like, you can warm a little more golden syrup in a pan and pour it over – or serve it with cream or custard.

Will's Steamed Treacle Sponge Pudding

Yorkshire Curd Tart

Yorkshire Curd Tart

The curd makes this tart lovely and moist, with a taste and texture you won't find in any other cake or pastry. It's perfect with morning coffee or afternoon tea.

Serves 8 15 mins preparation, 1 hr 15 mins cooking

Ingredients

110g unsalted butter, softened

75g caster sugar

Zest of ½ lemon, grated finely

1 egg, beaten

225g plain flour

1 pinch salt

25cm flan dish

Baking beans

For the curd filling

200g Yorkshire curd (available in selected stores)

100g unsalted butter

75g caster sugar

100g currants

1 egg, beaten

1 tablespoon brioche crumbs or soft breadcrumbs

Zest of 1 lemon, grated finely

Nutmeg, grated

To make the pastry

1. Mix the butter and sugar until smooth. Add the lemon zest and egg. Sieve the flour and salt, and add to the mixture.

2. Knead the dough lightly, wrap it in cling film, and let it rest in the fridge for an hour.

3. Preheat the oven to 160°C/gas mark 3.

4. Roll out the pastry to a 5mm thickness and use it to line a 25cm flan dish. Then the pastry needs to be baked blind. To do this, place a sheet of greaseproof paper over the pastry and fill with baking beans. Bake in the oven for 15 minutes or until all the visible pastry is thoroughly cooked.

To make the curd filling

1. Mix the butter and sugar together, then add the curd, well-beaten egg, brioche crumbs, currants and lemon zest.

2. Mix again very gently (if you over mix, it will break down the curds).

To finish the tart

1. Pour the filling into the flan dish, and sprinkle with lots of freshly grated nutmeg.

2. Bake in the oven for 50-60 minutes. Leave to cool before you serve.

Essentials

Dressings for salads. Sauces for pasta, meat
or fish. When you're short of time, it's useful
to have them already prepared in your fridge

Caesar Salad Dressing

Caesar Salad Dressing

This quick and easy dressing transforms a simple salad into something a little more special.

15 mins preparation

Ingredients
2 egg yolks
1 clove garlic
Juice of 1 lime
1 tablespoon mustard powder
A dash of Worcestershire sauce
150ml olive oil
50g Fresh Parmesan cheese, grated

1. Put the egg yolks, garlic, mustard powder, lime juice, Worcestershire sauce and Parmesan in a food processor.

2. Start the processor, and slowly drizzle in the olive oil until it's all blended.

3. Store in a jam jar or similar container in the fridge, for up to 5 days.

Guacamole and Salsa

Guacamole and Salsa

The perfect accompaniments for chilli con carne but also great party food, ideal for dipping with nachos.

30 mins preparation

Guacamole ingredients
Juice of 1 lime
1 small fresh chilli, finely chopped
½ red onion, chopped
1 clove garlic, crushed
3 ripe avocados, chopped
1 small bunch coriander, chopped
Sea salt and black pepper

Salsa ingredients
6 ripe tomatoes, skinned, de-seeded and chopped
1 small red onion
2 chillies, finely chopped
1 large bunch coriander, chopped
Juice of 1 lime
Sea salt and black pepper

To make the Guacamole

1. Mix all the ingredients together in a bowl. To stop the avocados browning, oil a piece of cling film and place it firmly over the guacamole.

2. Keep in the fridge and use the same day.

To make the Salsa

1. To remove the skins from the tomatoes, cross them lightly with a small knife, place in a large bowl and cover with boiling water. Leave for 12 seconds.

2. Using a spoon, take the tomatoes out of the hot water, plunge them into cold water, then peel off the skin. Cut in half, remove the seeds, and chop the tomato flesh.

3. Place in a bowl and mix in the remaining ingredients. Keep in the fridge and use the same day.

Pesto

The pesto you buy in the shops is okay – but for an authentic, fresh flavour, you can't beat this homemade recipe. Try it with pasta, chicken or fish.

20 mins preparation

Ingredients
50g toasted pine nuts
70g Fresh Parmesan cheese, grated
100ml olive oil
2 large bunches basil leaves
Ground black pepper
1 pinch rock salt

1. In a food processor, pulse the basil leaves, pine nuts and Parmesan.

2. Slowly add the olive oil until it forms a paste. Season with salt and pepper.

3. Keep your pesto in a jar in the fridge. If you want to keep it for up to two weeks,
   oil a piece of cling film and place it on top of the pesto before putting the lid on.

Pesto

Savoury Pudding

If you want a change from stuffing with your roast pork, try this recipe. It also goes really well with duck.

15 mins preparation, 1 hr soaking time and 35 mins cooking

Ingredients
275g white bread (crusts removed), cut into 2cm squares

150g suet

150g oatmeal

500ml milk

2 large onions, finely chopped

1 large bunch mixed fresh herbs (such as sage, thyme and parsley)

Zest of 1 lemon, grated

2 tablespoons mustard powder

2 eggs

Salt and pepper

Lined baking tray, 1cm thick

1. Soak the bread in the milk for an hour. Then squeeze out as much milk as possible, and discard the milk.

2. Preheat the oven to 180°C/gas mark 4.

3. Using an electric mixer, blend all the ingredients together until well combined. Spread onto a lined baking tray to a thickness of 1cm. Bake for 35 minutes or until golden brown.

Savoury Pudding

Tomato Sauce for Pasta

Tomato Sauce for Pasta

Pasta sauce in a jar is often a disappointment. I think it's worth just a little effort to make it yourself.

10 mins preparation, 40 mins cooking

Ingredients
4 shallots, chopped
4 cloves garlic, chopped
2 tablespoons olive oil
2 star anise
4 x 400g tins chopped tomatoes
50ml red wine vinegar
2 tablespoons caster sugar
Salt and pepper

To serve
Pasta
Fresh basil leaves
Fresh Parmesan cheese, grated
Olive oil

1. Gently heat the oil in a pan and cook the shallots and garlic until they're soft, but not brown.

2. Add the tinned tomatoes and star anise, then cook gently for 40 minutes.

3. In a small pan, heat the vinegar and sugar until boiling, and then add this to the tomato sauce. Season with salt and pepper.

4. To serve, spoon the sauce over freshly cooked pasta. Drizzle with olive oil, and top with fresh basil leaves and grated Parmesan.

5. If you don't want to use the sauce immediately, let it cool and keep it in a sealed jar in the fridge for up to two weeks.

Vinaigrette

Vinaigrette

This homemade vinaigrette is a quick way to liven up a salad – and you can keep it handy in the fridge.

10 mins preparation

Ingredients
300ml olive oil
300ml rapeseed oil
125ml white wine vinegar
Juice of 1 lemon
1 tablespoon fresh thyme
1 tablespoon Dijon mustard
2 shallots, chopped
2 cloves garlic, chopped
1 tablespoon caster sugar
Salt and pepper

1. Blend all the ingredients in a liquidiser. Check the seasoning, and pour into a clean wine bottle or similar container. Store in the fridge for up to one month.

2. Shake well before serving.

Yorkshire Pudding

Yorkshire Pudding

Yorkshire pudding recipes can be quite controversial. Everybody thinks theirs is the best one – and of course, I think mine is too! I add a little mustard for extra flavour, which works brilliantly with roast beef.

Makes 12 small or 6 large Yorkshire puddings
(depending on the type of tray you use)
10 mins preparation, 25 mins cooking

Ingredients
3 eggs
115g plain flour
275ml milk
1 dessert spoon English mustard powder
Beef dripping
Salt and pepper

1. Preheat the oven to 200°C/gas mark 6.

2. Sieve the flour and mustard powder into a large bowl. Beat the eggs in a separate bowl, then add to the flour and beat again, gradually adding the milk as you beat. Season with salt and pepper.

3. Put a Yorkshire pudding tray into the oven to heat. When it's hot, take it out and add about 1 tablespoon of beef dripping, sharing it between the cavities. Return it to the oven for several minutes, until the fat is smoking hot.

4. Carefully remove the tray from the oven. Then use a ladle to pour the batter mixture into each cavity, filling each one to two thirds. Return to the oven for 15-20 minutes, or until the puddings are well risen and golden. Serve immediately.

Lamona Appliance, Sink and Tap Collection

Exclusive to Howdens Joinery, and selected to perfectly complement our range of kitchens, Lamona appliances offer outstanding levels of reliability and performance, from our entry level products right through to our highest specification models. Each is manufactured to the highest standards of durability, and built to use less energy and water, and run quietly whilst giving excellent value for money.

You can choose from ovens, range cookers, microwaves, hobs, extractors, fridges, freezers, dishwashers, washing machines, tumble dryers, sinks and taps, which are all designed to fit beautifully into your Howdens kitchen.

You will have the reassurance that we supply 500,000 appliances and 590,000 sinks and taps each year to UK homes.

All Lamona appliances come with a 12 month manufacturer's warranty and what we believe is the best after sales service in the UK.

Lamona products are available from stock in 490 local depots to your trade professional. To find out more and for detailed product specifications, please refer to **www.lamona.co.uk**

Exclusive to Howdens Joinery Co.

The General Tarleton

An old coaching inn with contemporary comforts, The General Tarleton Inn is in the pretty village of Ferrensby close to both York and Harrogate. Owned and run by John and Claire Topham for the past 12 years, The General Tarleton is constantly evolving but always sticks to the basic philosophy of offering great service and excellent food and drink in a relaxed atmosphere, and if you are staying the night, a comfortable room to rest your head.

The focus is on food

In The General Tarleton kitchen, John heads an experienced and dedicated team. Menus change daily to reflect the seasons and the pick of the catch or crop that day. John gets a call most days from the fishing boats as they return to port and within hours the fish is in the kitchen. Yorkshire has an abundance of excellent suppliers, which The General Tarleton has worked with over the years to obtain the very best seasonal produce.

The General Tarleton Inn, Boroughbridge Road, Ferrensby, Knaresborough, HG5 0PZ
Tel 01423 340284 www.generaltarleton.co.uk